AUGUSTA READ THOMAS

T0210309

SIX PIANO ETUDES

(1996-2005)

ED 4289
First Printing September 2006

ISBN-13: 978-1-4234-1242-7

G. SCHIRMER, Inc.

DISTRIBUTED BY

HAL•LEONARD®
CORPORATION
7777 W. BLUEMOUND RD. P.O. BOX 13819 MILWAUKEE, WI 53213

Composer's Note

The aim of my piano etudes, which are composed in pairs, is to create drastically different sonic effects for each, using musical material identical to both. They should be like looking at two sides of a coin or examining both a photograph and its negative. These six small pieces were carefully heard, built, and refined, and as a result took a long time to compose.

I. *Orbital Beacons* is about rotating harmonies and glow. The work juxtaposes very loud notes with very soft ones, making a counterpoint of layers and implied voice leading in which at first there are more soft notes than loud ones; by the end of the piece, this has been reversed. The work, which should sound clean, natural, and colorful, is highly organized. It is about the beauty of resonance, echo, decay, and luminosity.

II. *Fire Waltz* is a variation on Etude N°· I, in which the notes that were loud are strung together, exactly in order, lowered by two octaves, and turned into a boogie woogie bass line. The notes that were soft in Etude N°· I form Bartók-like, jazzy chords. Although I think it is easy to hear the many references to perfumes of jazz in all my music, here is a work where the scents are more explicit. All the influences in my music are highly digested and personalized; for instance in these first two etudes we can sense Debussy, Ravel, Webern, and Berio, in addition to jazz, but hopefully the music is "all Thomas," and not stolen Debussy for instance, nor a display of simpleminded piano clichés.

III. *Cathedral Waterfall* is a slow unfolding of the series of rich chords of an extended jazz harmony idiom. The color of each chord is precise and individual. One can imagine a huge, dramatic cathedral carillon where many bells are being rung at once, making beautiful complex chords that hang in the air, and echo, while at the same time, there is one lone bell ringer who is out of synchronization with the tutti chords. In the end the chord rolls slowly downward, like a waterfall of chimes, and fades away, leaving only the ringing of two last bells.

IV. *On Twilight* is two and a half minutes of high energy. The three distinct layers crosscut one another in unpredictable, edgy, hiccup-like fits and starts, like a jazz improvisation that gets "out of the box." Yet, there is always the central "on twilight" layer flickering along, like the sun beaming, glowing, bursting, and then setting slowly into twilight. The outer two layers, in the two most extreme registers of the piano suggest the emergence of everything else in the evening cosmos (stars, planets, galaxies, black holes, etc.), which come into view only at twilight, as the sun sets and fades over the horizon.

V. *Rain At Funeral* is an impressionist miniature funeral march, which requires very subtle shadings in quiet dynamics as well as in timbre and reverberation. It uses the exact same chords as Etude N°· VI and is purposely a very intricate, delicate, private etude, in contrast to the bravura flair of its surrounding etudes, N°ˢ· IV and VI.

VI. *Twitter-Machines* was composed in homage to David Rakowski, a world-class composer, who has written a large number of stellar piano etudes. *Twitter-Machines* responds to Rakowski's first etude, *E-Machines*, in which single notes are repeated very quickly. My etude repeats chords of various shapes and sizes as quickly as possible and these twittering chords are often interrupted by grace-note figures (anywhere from one to nine grace notes), which are played on the beat and which "mess-up the pulse," thus forcing the pianist to be slightly late for the main notes that follow. As the repeated chords delineate a certain tight bandwidth of pitch, florid arabesques that cover the entire range of the piano are set in relief against those oscillating machinelike harmonies.

—Augusta Read Thomas

Duration ca. 17 minutes

Etudes I and II (1996) were commissioned by Judy Kehler Siebert,
to whom they are dedicated with admiration,
and who gave their first performance on 20 March 1997,
at Brock University, St. Catherines, Ontario, Canada.
A recording of Etudes I and II by members of the Society for New Music
is available on Innova; CD616 (Amerian Masters for the 21st Century).

Etudes III and IV (2003) were commissioned by the American Pianists Association,
through the Christel Award, for 1995 Classical Fellow James Giles,
to whom they are dedicated, and who presented their first performances;
11 April 2003 in Indianapolis, 16 April 2003 at Wigmore Hall, London,
and 19 April 2003 at the Sibelius Academy, Helsinki.
Mr. Giles has recorded Etudes I-IV on Albany Records: TROY860.

Etudes V and VI (2005) were co-premiered by
Amy Dissanayake on 3 March 2006,
at Ganz Hall, Roosevelt University, Chicago, Illinois,
and by Stephen Gosling on 23 March 2006,
at Merkin Hall, New York City.

SIX PIANO ETUDES

(1996–2005)

Augusta Read Thomas

for Judy Kehler Siebert

I. Orbital Beacons–Homage to Luciano Berio

Damper pedal *sempre* ⟶
U.C. pedal *sempre* (but use only on the **pp** figures, not on the **sffz** notes) ⟶

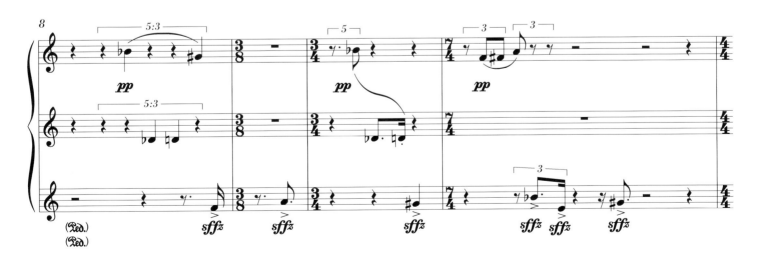

4

II. Fire Waltz–Homage to Béla Bartók

Perpetual motion–Bartók boogie-woogie ♩ = 132

for James Giles

III. Cathedral Waterfall–Homage to Olivier Messiaen

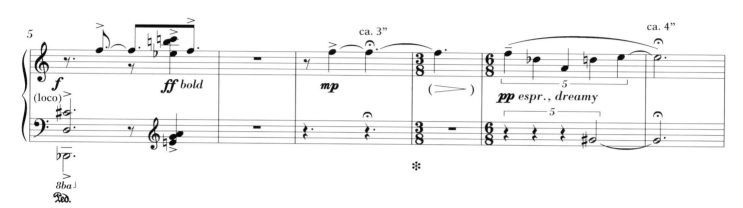

*Tempo can be flexible. Slower
  in the quieter music and faster
  in the louder music.
**Bar 2 must be louder than bar 1

*Ped. down just after the attack

attaca optional

for James Giles

IV. On Twilight–Homage to Pierre Boulez

*Tempo can be flexible; faster end of this range is preferred.

N.B.: Use very little damper pedal throughout this etude.

V. Rain At Funeral–Homage to Morton Feldman

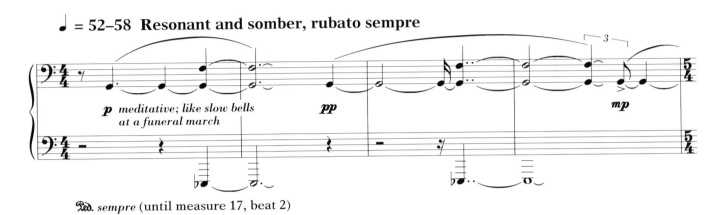

♩ = 52–58 **Resonant and somber, rubato sempre**

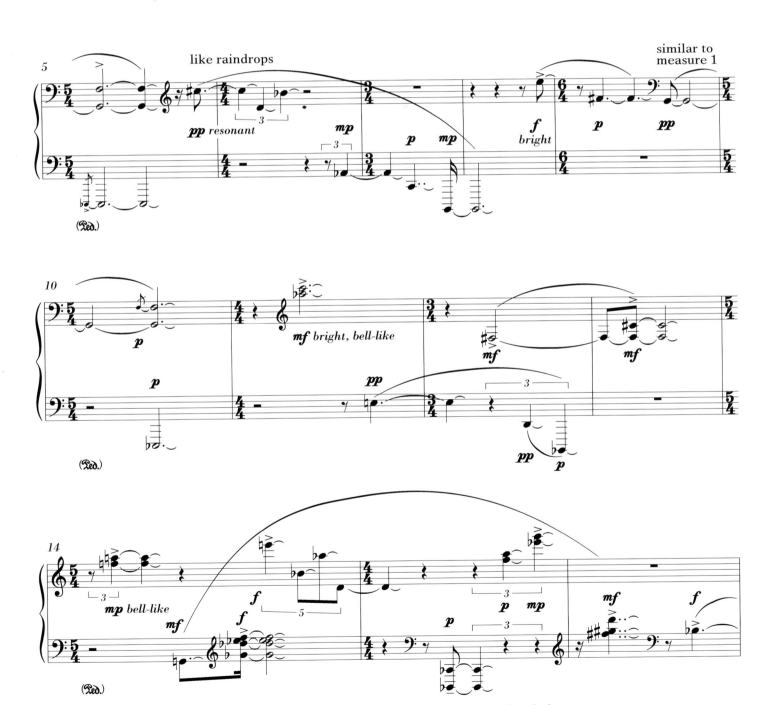

Note: Despite the often rising lines, this etude should feel as if it is always pulling downward to the low notes.

VI. Twitter-Machines–Homage to David Rakowski

♩ = 120; or, **As fast as possible**, if 120 is too fast (tempo **should** be variable and does **not** have to be stable from measure to measure. This will add to a "twittering" and "jazzy" effect.)

Note: 1) It is intended that the pianist must divide between the two hands all the repeated notes in the manner he/she most prefers. This is for a particular color as well as for the tempi.

    2) All grace notes come before the beat. They are allowed, and supposed, to "mess up" the pulse, so that what follows them can be slightly late.

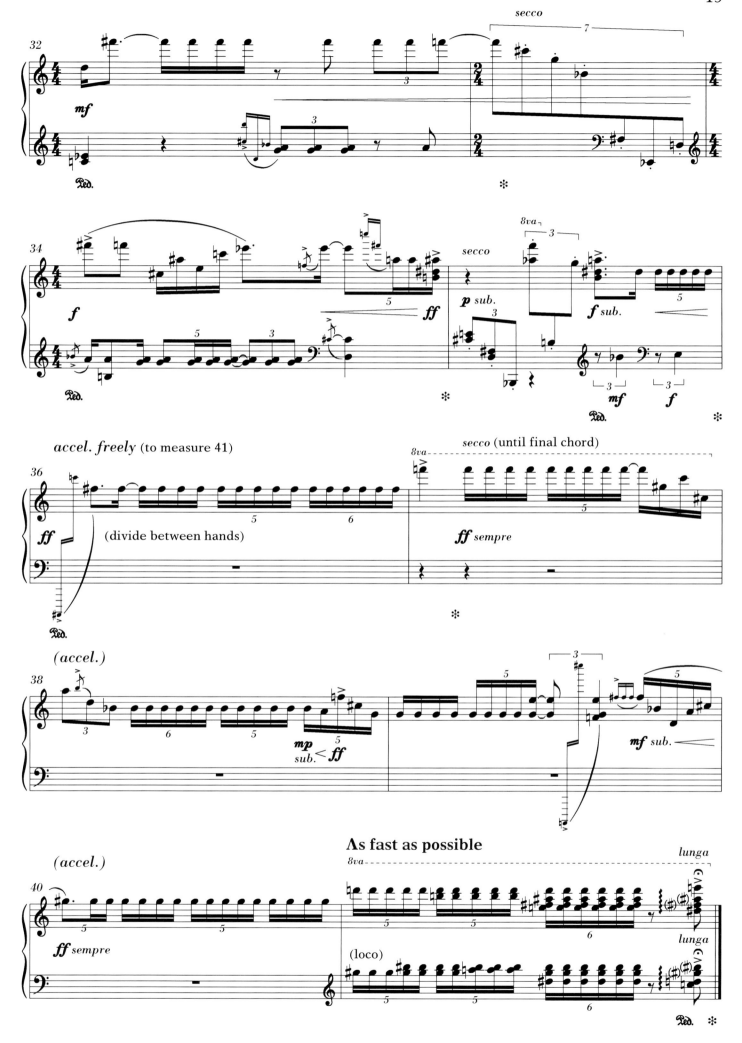